Is the Treat Sour or Sweet?

Mary Elizabeth Salzmann

Consulting Editor, Diane Craig, M.A./Reading Specialist

ABDO
Publishing Company

Published by ABDO Publishing Company, 4940 Viking Drive, Edina, Minnesota 55435.

Printed in the United States.

Credits
Edited by: Pam Price
Curriculum Coordinator: Nancy Tuminelly
Cover and Interior Design and Production: Mighty Media
Photo Credits: BananaStock Ltd., Creatas, Image100, Purestock, ShutterStock, Wewerka Photography

Library of Congress Cataloging-in-Publication Data
Salzmann, Mary Elizabeth, 1968-
  Is the treat sour or sweet? / Mary Elizabeth Salzmann.
     p. cm. -- (Antonyms)
  ISBN-13: 978-1-59928-719-5
  ISBN-10: 1-59928-719-6
  1. English language--Synonyms and antonyms--Juvenile literature. I. Title.

PE1591.S268 2007
428.1--dc22
                           2006032020

SandCastle™ books are created by a professional team of educators, reading specialists, and content developers around five essential components—phonemic awareness, phonics, vocabulary, text comprehension, and fluency—to assist young readers as they develop reading skills and strategies and increase their general knowledge. All books are written, reviewed, and leveled for guided reading, early reading intervention, and Accelerated Reader® programs for use in shared, guided, and independent reading and writing activities to support a balanced approach to literacy instruction.

Let Us Know

SandCastle would like to hear your stories about reading this book. What is your favorite page? Was there something hard that you needed help with? Share the ups and downs of learning to read. We want to hear from you! To get posted on the ABDO Publishing Company Web site, send us e-mail at:

sandcastle@abdopublishing.com

SandCastle Level: Transitional

Antonyms are words that have opposite meanings.

Here is a good way to remember what an antonym is:

antonym

=

opposite

Also, **antonym** and **opposite** both start with vowels.

3

antonyms

Madison's lemon tastes sour.

antonyms

Daniel's candy bar tastes sweet.

antonyms

Jacob's apple is hard.

Ashley's watermelon is soft.

antonyms

The vegetables in Isabella's salad are raw.

Michael's pizza is cooked.

Andrew's slice of cheese is thin.

Olivia's cheeseburger is thick.

antonyms

Christopher eats a
cold ice-cream cone
on a hot summer day.

antonyms

The bowl is full of spaghetti. After Samantha's family finishes dinner, the bowl will be empty.

antonyms

The ice cubes in Ryan's drink were frozen, but now most of them are melted.

antonyms

Elizabeth and her mom are baking a fresh loaf of bread. They will put it in a plastic bag so it will not get stale.

Antonym Activity

cold   hot

sour   sweet

hard   soft

empty   full

Antonym Pairs

cold — hot

cooked — raw

empty — full

fresh — stale

frozen — melted

hard — soft

sour — sweet

thick — thin

In each box on page 20, choose the antonym that describes the picture.

Words I Know

Nouns
A noun is a person, place, or thing.

apple, 6
bag, 19
bowl, 15
bread, 19
candy bar, 5
cheese, 10
cheeseburger, 11
day, 13

dinner, 15
drink, 17
family, 15
ice-cream cone, 13
ice cubes, 17
lemon, 4
loaf, 19
mom, 19

pizza, 9
salad, 8
slice, 10
spaghetti, 15
vegetables, 8
watermelon, 7

Adjectives
An adjective describes something.

cold, 13
cooked, 9
empty, 15
fresh, 19
frozen, 17
full, 15
hard, 6

her, 19
hot, 13
melted, 17
most, 17
plastic, 19
raw, 8
soft, 7

sour, 4
stale, 19
summer, 13
sweet, 5
thick, 11
thin, 10

Words I Know

Verbs
A verb is an action or being word.

are, 8, 17, 19
baking, 19
be, 15
eats, 13

finishes, 15
get, 19
is, 6, 7, 9, 10, 11, 15
put, 19

tastes, 4, 5
were, 17
will, 15, 19

Proper Nouns
A proper noun is the name of a person, place, or thing.

Andrew, 10
Ashley, 7
Christopher, 13
Daniel, 5

Elizabeth, 19
Isabella, 8
Jacob, 6
Madison, 4

Michael, 9
Olivia, 11
Ryan, 17
Samantha, 15

About SandCastle™

A professional team of educators, reading specialists, and content developers created the SandCastle™ series to support young readers as they develop reading skills and strategies and increase their general knowledge. The SandCastle™ series has four levels that correspond to early literacy development in young children. The levels are provided to help teachers and parents select appropriate books for young readers.

Emerging Readers
(no flags)

Beginning Readers
(1 flag)

Transitional Readers
(2 flags)

Fluent Readers
(3 flags)

These levels are meant only as a guide. All levels are subject to change.

To see a complete list of SandCastle™ books and other nonfiction titles from ABDO Publishing Company, visit www.abdopublishing.com or contact us at:
4940 Viking Drive, Edina, Minnesota 55435 • 1-800-800-1312 • fax: 1-952-831-1632